Joanie Boney Books

www.joanieboneybooks.com

Lucky lived with her parents,
who were farmers.

They lived in a beautiful village that had wonderful meadows filled with flowers and trees and insects flying around.

Near the river, bumblebees were always gathering and flying from flower to flower.

Lucky loved to go there and chase the bumblebees.

She would talk about their fat, yellow bodies, and about their short wings, and their big, beautiful eyes.

One day, when she went down by the river, she saw that there were not as many bumblebees as usual. Lucky said to herself, "Where are all the bumblebees?"

And those that were there were flying slowly. She went closer to them and saw some bumblebees lying on the soft grass, trying to fly.

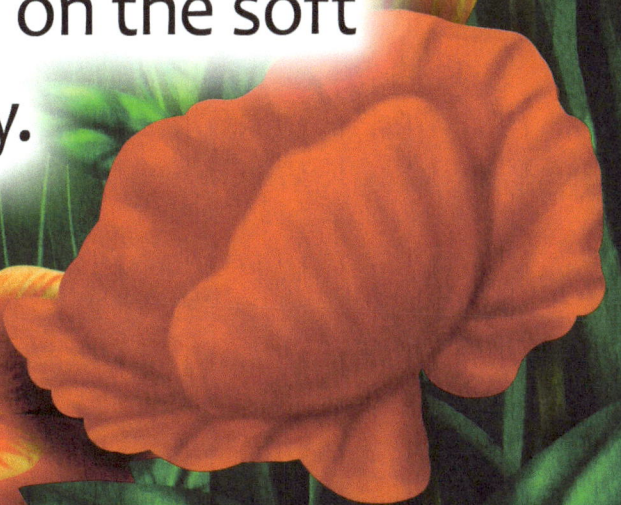

She ran to her father and said, "Daddy, the bumblebees are very sick." She couldn't understand what was happening, why the bumblebees were sick.

She started crying and asking, "What's wrong with them? What made them sick?" Her father asked her to show him the place where the bumblebees were gathered.

When they got there, she asked him what was wrong and he told her that this was the place where most of the farmers were disposing of their chemicals. He said, "These chemicals are very bad for the bumblebees, Lucky."

Lucky understood that those chemicals were harmful to the bumblebees and she knew she had to do something about it.

When she got home she took some paper and crayons, and started drawing and writing something on paper.

She drew beautiful, yellow bumblebees and flowers and wrote some words.

When she was done with the drawing and writing, she took the paper to her father. He was in the barn, working with some tools, and she gave him the paper and asked him to put it on a wooden stick.

She said, "Daddy, would you help me put the posters all around for people to read and stop using bad chemicals that are hurting the bumblebees?"

Her father was so proud of
her, and hugged her.

Afterwards, Lucky took her toy shovel and went to the meadow near the river where the chemicals were.

Save the Bumblebees

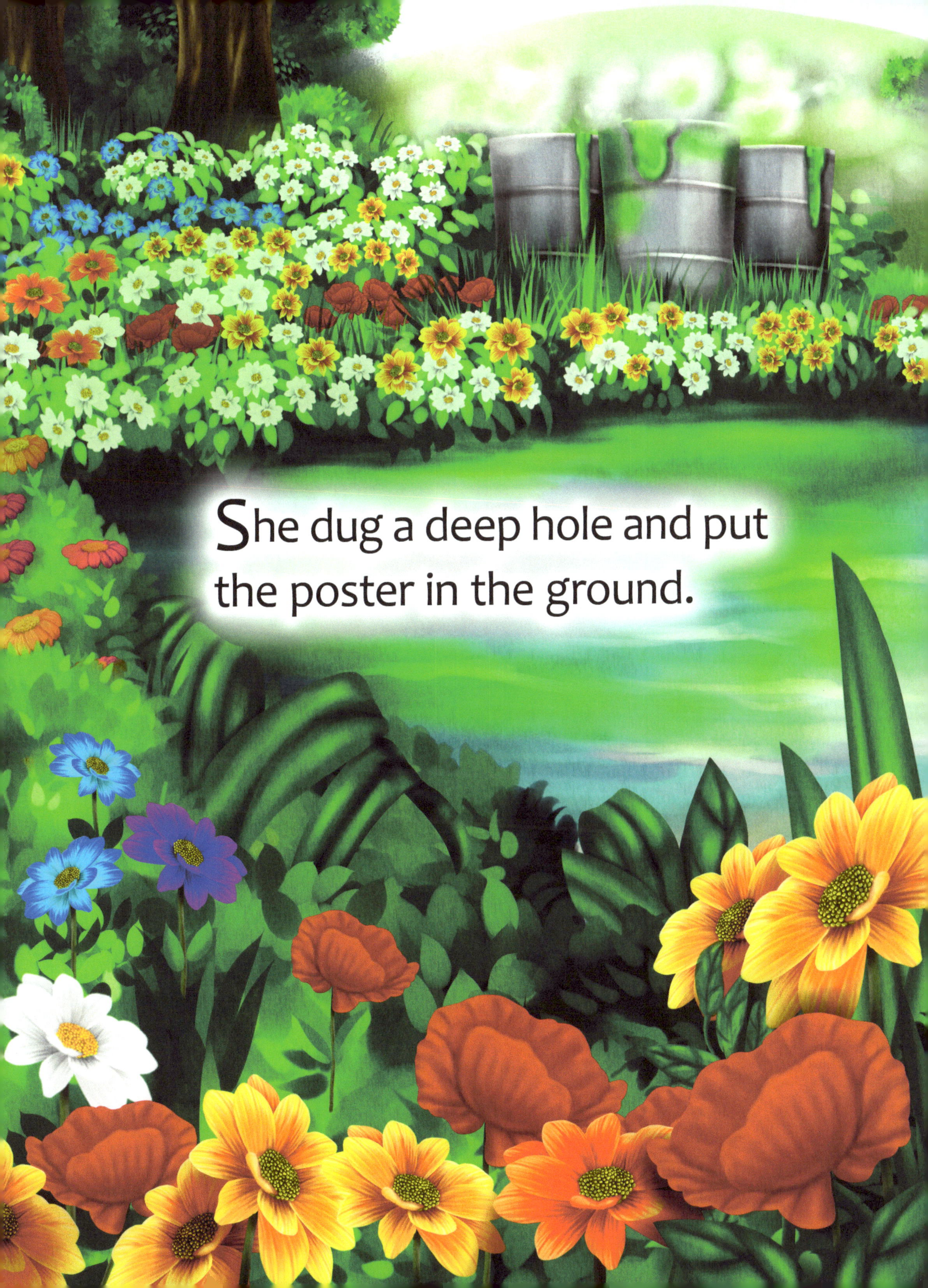

She dug a deep hole and put the poster in the ground.

The next morning, everyone was talking about the signs that were posted.

They asked around and found out that Lucky was the one who posted them. They were so proud of her.

Lucky told them that they should all try to help the bumblebees, save them, not hurt them.

She told them that they should plant more pretty flowers and apple trees and cherry trees and peach trees.

She suggested they plant more blueberry bushes and let the bumblebees make them more beautiful.

Lucky told them how much she loved the bumblebees and how much the bumblebees loved them and made the world a better place.

When she finished her speech everyone applauded her.

Later that week, Lucky was surprised when she went to the meadow near the river. There she saw that all the chemicals had been removed. And hundreds of bumblebees were flying happily around and she could chase them again.